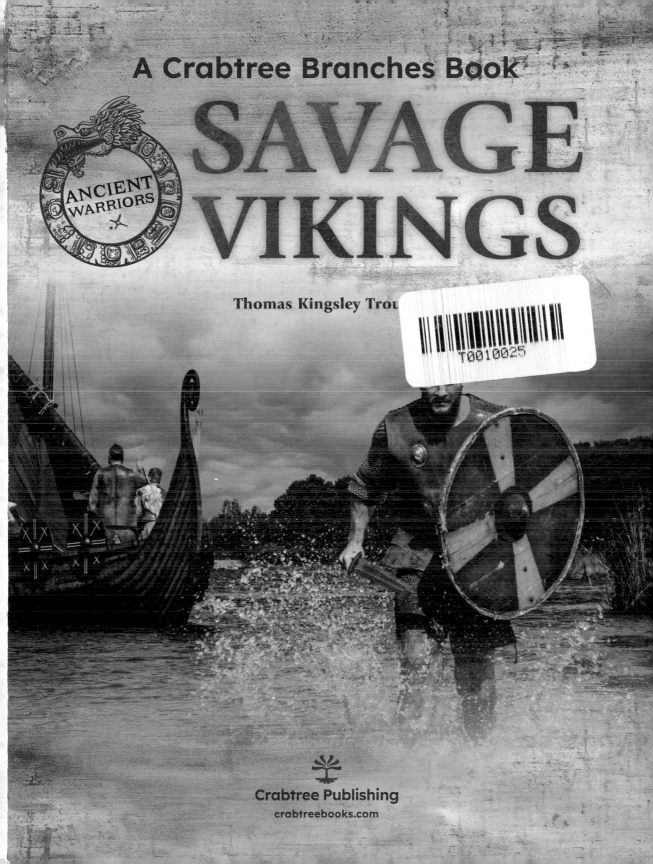

A Crabtree Branches Book

SAVAGE VIKINGS

ANCIENT WARRIORS

Thomas Kingsley Trou

T0010025

Crabtree Publishing
crabtreebooks.com

School-to-Home Support for Caregivers and Teachers

This high-interest book is designed to motivate striving students with engaging topics while building fluency, vocabulary, and an interest in reading. Here are a few questions and activities to help the reader build upon his or her comprehension skills.

Before Reading:

- *What do I think this book is about?*
- *What do I know about this topic?*
- *What do I want to learn about this topic?*
- *Why am I reading this book?*

During Reading:

- *I wonder why...*
- *I'm curious to know...*
- *How is this like something I already know?*
- *What have I learned so far?*

After Reading:

- *What was the author trying to teach me?*
- *What are some details?*
- *How did the photographs and captions help me understand more?*
- *Read the book again and look for the vocabulary words.*
- *What questions do I still have?*

Extension Activities:

- *What was your favorite part of the book? Write a paragraph on it.*
- *Draw a picture of your favorite thing you learned from the book.*

TABLE OF CONTENTS

On a Raid

The Viking warrior stands at the **bow** of the longship. The boat glides silently down the river, heading toward the village along the shore.

Men grumble as the ship gets closer. When they are yards from the beach, one of them blows into a horn. The villagers scramble. The Viking raid has begun!

What's a Viking?

Vikings were people from Scandinavia, an area that today includes Sweden, Norway, and Denmark. Sometimes called Norsemen, Vikings were known as great warriors and seamen.

Vikings were raiders, traders, pirates, explorers, and **colonizers**. People who lived in nearby countries lived in terror of the Vikings.

Fun Fact

The word Viking comes from the Old Norse word *vikingr*, which was believed to mean "pirate" or "raider."

A large number of Scandinavians left their homelands from about 800 C.E. into the 11th century. They wanted to find new lands that were suitable for farming.

Coming from different parts of Scandinavia, they were a mixed group of Danes, Swedes, and Norwegians. These **nomadic** people became the Vikings.

Viking History & Life

Some believe the Viking Age started in 793 C.E. A group of Vikings from Norway raided the Lindisfarne **monastery** in Northeastern England.

The Vikings stole valuable objects from the monastery, but did not destroy it. The attack left the people scared. If the Vikings robbed churches, they would steal from anyone.

When Vikings weren't raiding and exploring, most were farmers. Others were craftsmen who made weapons and built ships.

The large structures Vikings lived in were called longhouses. The longships they built for raids and exploring used both sails and oars.

Viking longhouses were huge and resembled upside-down longships. As many as 30 to 50 people could live inside a longhouse. Many families and multiple **generations** shared the space.

Viking Clothing

When Vikings weren't in battle, they wore simple clothes. They needed to be comfortable when they worked on the farm or in a workshop.

Men wore a tunic, which is like a long shirt. They also wore trousers and a cloak. A Viking woman often wore a strap dress, which looked like an apron, over top of a smock.

Vikings who set out on raids needed to wear clothing to protect themselves. Warriors wore helmets made of iron or leather if they could afford it.

Fun Fact

Vikings didn't actually have horns on their helmets. An opera in 1870 featured actors playing Vikings. They wore horned helmets in the production and the image stuck.

They wore armor made of **chainmail** or possibly leather armor, called *lamellar*, to protect their **torsos**. Poorer Vikings wore layers of quilted cloth.

Viking Weapons

Raiding villages and churches is dangerous business. Vikings brought all kinds of weapons to their raids. The richer the Viking, the better quality were his weapons.

Common Vikings fought with a spear and shield. Wealthy Vikings had those, plus a sword. All Vikings carried a *seax*, which was a small **dagger**.

Fun Fact

Swords were very important to some Vikings. Many handed down their sword to a son. Sometimes Vikings wanted to be buried with their weapons after they died.

Vikings fought with a bow and arrow when they were at sea as well as in land battles. Whether hunting animals or fighting people, the same bow was used.

Axes were another multiple-use tool and weapon. Many trees and enemies were felled with their blades. Some axes were so large, it took two hands to **wield** them.

Viking Fighting

Unlike a lot of warriors throughout history, Vikings didn't fight on horseback. They preferred to fight on the ground, head to head with their enemies.

At that time, England did not have a navy to patrol its coasts. Many Viking raids came by river or by sea. The Vikings would jump from their boats upon landing and quickly attack.

Fun Fact

Vikings loved boats. A fallen warrior was often honored by being buried in a funeral boat. They would place the body in new clothes, surround him with his weapons, and cover the boat with dirt.

Viking raids and combat were brutal. Not only did Vikings steal from the villages they raided, they sometimes destroyed them too.

Many villages were burned down after the Vikings took what they wanted. No one was safe during a Viking attack. Men, women, and even children were all in danger when Vikings raided.

Vikings Today

The Viking Age ended in 1066 when the last Viking king, Harald Hardrada, was killed. He and his army were defeated in the Battle of Stamford Bridge in England.

The Vikings had colonized so many distant lands, their **descendants** continued to have influence, even under new rulers. They settled down to a normal life in places like Northern England, Scotland, and Russia.

Fun Fact

The Vikings worshiped many gods. The main gods were Odin, Thor, and Freya. Odin was the god of war, Thor was the god of thunder, and Freya was the goddess of **fertility**.

Even today, their influence is found in our use of Viking words and place names. Viking **mythology** and tales of their seafaring conquests still fascinate us.

Although the Vikings gained huge wealth from being the greatest traders of their time, they are best known for their bloody raids. The Vikings will always be remembered as bold and savage warriors!

Glossary

bow (BOU) The forward part of a ship

chainmail (CHAYN-mayl) Armor made of small metal rings linked together in a pattern to form a mesh of small chains

colonizers (KAA-luh-nai-zrz) People who take control of an area or a country that is not their own, often using force

dagger (DA-gr) A short weapon for stabbing

descendants (dih-SEN-duhntz) People who are related to a person or people who lived before

fertility (fr-TI-luh-tee) The ability to produce children

generations (jeh-nr-AY-shnz) All of the people born and living around the same time

monastery (MAA-nuh-steh-ree) A holy place where monks or nuns live and work

mythology (mi-THOL-uh-jee) A collection of traditional tales called myths from a particular culture

nomadic (now-MAD-ik) Describing people who move from place to place, not living in a permanent area

torso (TAWR-soh) The middle part of the body

wield (WEELD) To handle or use

Index

Websites to Visit

https://www.youtube.com/watch?v=UpxIGTvKwOE
[Video about the history of the Vikings]

https://www.funkidslive.com/learn/top-10-facts/top-10-facts-about-vikings/

https://historyforkids.org/the-vikings-facts-for-kids/

About the Author

Thomas Kingsley Troupe is the author of over 200 books for young readers. When he's not writing, he enjoys reading, playing video games, and investigating haunted places with the Twin Cities Paranormal Society. Otherwise, he's probably taking a nap or something. Thomas lives in Woodbury, Minnesota, with his two sons.

Written by: Thomas Kingsley Troupe
Designed by: Bobbie Houser
Series Development: James Earley
Proofreader: Kathy Middleton
Educational Consultant: Marie Lemke M.Ed.

Photographs:
Shutterstock: Nejron Photo: cover, p. 1, 4-5, 9, 20, 22-23, 28-29; DanieleGay: p. 6-7; vlastas: p. 8; DigitalAssetArt: p. 10-11; ricochet64: p. 12-13; faestock: p. 14; Valentina Zavgorodniaia: p. 15; Denis Gorlach: p. 16; Fotokvadrat: p. 17, 21, 26-27; FXQuadro: p. 18-19; Nomad_Soul: p. 24-25

Crabtree Publishing

crabtreebooks.com   800-387-7650
Copyright © 2024 Crabtree Publishing

Printed in the U.S.A./072023/CG20230214

Published in Canada
Crabtree Publishing
616 Welland Ave.
St. Catharines, Ontario
L2M 5V6

Published in the United States
Crabtree Publishing
347 Fifth Ave
Suite 1402-145
New York, NY 10016

Library and Archives Canada Cataloguing in Publication
Available at Library and Archives Canada

Library of Congress Cataloging-in-Publication Data
Available at the Library of Congress

Hardcover: 978-1-0398-0949-9
Paperback: 978-1-0398-1002-0
Ebook (pdf): 978-1-0398-1108-9
Epub: 978-1-0398-1055-6